Piece

By

Peace

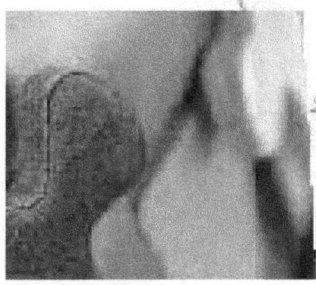

INTRODUCTION

I found myself I must say So now all my thoughts once again I start writing away this Title I
share is from lifes blessings as well as lessons learned As I visualize all the yesterdays into today.with an open mind I love to see the positive picture in every setting in life and knowing the greatest is love and optimism staying well focused on the brighter pieces of allowing a door opening of much peace.

Piece by peace

As the sun starts to slowly pass through the clouds bringing in the evening fresh cool air. I lay for a moment to take it all in while laying on my pillow and my head to the window feeling the breeze and thinking how fast the days pass us through. Searching in my thoughts really of "why am I here: what are Gods plans for me to do HERE?

While some wake up each morning with same routines and often having plans. Some may not but, to only maybe make a change of something new. Or just maybe to face something uninspected to rearrange or arrange something new. Still seeking for what's not yet been found. Or just to take a new peak all around finding great happiness instead of the head always hanging down.

I can say each day is sure to be different anyway rather just a little or a whole lot. Some very happy and quite peaceful while some can sure be sad some just like to worry I must say. Yes they do. Just waiting for anything negative to pass their way ,while many just keep a smile in   in spite of A struggle .So by the end of the day you always know all is ok and that is a piece to remember for it is a thought of peace that will   later fit life's puzzle

As I stare out the window and breath in the fresh cut green grass   and the many lilac flowers. And you know some people could just stay in bed for hours. Not wanting to get on with another day thinking of all the work they must do or just missing the one who went away.

It's all ok though you know just knowing there really is a new day even when you don't feel so into it. Just believe in God and pray.

Living by faith all makes perfect sense to me more and more as years go by. As we can grow in wisdom passing through life's journey of some sunny days and some days darkened.

It was a beautiful summer day as the down hearted woman went on her morning stroll. Trying to enjoy the day but and in spite of her sadness she as always could carry enough hope in her heart that her faith in God could always override any negativity through her every train of thought that would be of any discouragement to her own thoughts.

AS she was walking along and passed the place where she would walk by quite often of seeing the three well, sometimes four horses through the chain linked fence. Well on this day she did stop as sometimes before but, just a longer visit than ever before. Just staring at the one singled out beautiful horse and with it staring back at her into one another's eyes through the holes of the linked fence.

The woman still feeling somewhat down hearted still in thoughts of A young man's plan for his own journey while looking in the eyes of the Beautiful horse she began to pray to God and saying help the young man find his destiny with many abilities yet some struggles he had. The woman thought as she pray maybe God "do you suppose he could ride horses someday? "SURLY! No man wants to stay home all-day. And the horse starred and her eyes as if he understood and was sharing the message in prayer along with the woman.

The woman now turns with a spiritual uplift in her soul now to walk back home. Not thinking anymore of anything basically still yet not knowing what tomorrow will bring. Only to know that hope that lives   with every piece of her heart. Knowing again that all the pieces of life day to day would not be or have to be just so perfect even though, with much pray and belief. God showers us with his love giving much peace on our saddest moments in his time

It never is understood clearly today of why things may not go the perfect ways   it   sure will make perfect sense tomorrow you know. Our lives sometimes seem to be as a big puzzle   we try to fit the pieces in order making our plans, settling with routines;   Living day to day .yet some people not having much of a routine or anything at all. No dreams or goals   some just don't want to do anything at all. Many just love to live fully in the past while some just love to remember and look at the future wrapping it altogether. Knowing there is always a better way especially when it's Gods way. And we sure know it is and that's always the better way anyways right?

A new morning now here and the little woman enjoys her cup of coffee as she starts her laundry and hanging the clothes across the clothesline to dry from the fresh breeze

Hearing the loud ringing of the rather old fashioned phone out in the yard coming from the kitchen window .Miss Smith walks briskly inside to answer. Now to hear the woman on the other end invites her to a meeting regarding the young man. To whom she's been hoping for a   perfect plan just out of high school.

A few days now passed to reach the day of the meeting .those were the longest three days ever. The woman and young man sat at a big table with two more in seating with them. As the elderly man with rather large glasses and a caring smile points out some job opportunities with the woman and young man briefly. In with which was One being woodworking and the other being A Stableman. Yes! As the woman is listening closely although, she falls into A moment of daydream   reminiscing the prayer and the horse the day of the morning stroll. The woman felt the blessing in her heart and kind of shocking but really not so very shocking because, of the faith she did have and this is just a awesome piece of life's journey of a peaceful moment to fit not only of today but , of yesterday's prayer that is   in action today

Yes the young man was hired as a stableman after learning how it would be and enjoying every day of his care giving as well as earning extra income. Today he cares for many horses. Now just a little shy of seven years at the place he is employed. And each day he stands in front of the eyes of a horse; God sure is there to of course.

A beautiful Saturday morning now here again .Miss Smith listens to the nearby sparrows sing outside her bedroom window just as the sun starts to rise. She stretches her arms up high and sits on the edge of her bed to slip the rather small pink slippers on her feet .Thinking of a brand new day to start and all the household chores to be accomplished. She pulls back her curtains in thoughts of maybe starting her Saturday outside in caring for her yard and many colorful flowers like   impatience and such. Watering them with her large silver watering can is what she likes to do.

Thinking of all the many things she needs to do and finish inside and out she decides to start her routine on the inside .Not allowing herself to get overwhelmed but, to ask the Lord for patience as she does her best to get everything done. Reminding herself she can always just water the flowers in the evening

Miss Smith is at her small table by her kitchen window just finishing her last taste of morning coffee. Now gathering up all her cleaning linens to wash up her white woodwork all around she slightly bends down   and starts scrubbing away with some help of her deepest elbow grease to shine her woodwork, along with a touch the fresh smelling pine cleaner.

Miss Smith suddenly hears a loud roar of thunder, causing her to just about   hit her own head on the corner of the table from the loud shocking sound. As she started off the floor she's scrubbing, than to look out at the pouring   rain and with a grateful smile in thanks to God for the rain, now she continued to accomplish her inside chores. Knowing the outside is now mostly finished .now this is a well fitted piece of that day bring much peace again.

The woman once fell in love with a handsome Man the first moment he took her hand. When she looked deep in those eyes the love they felt was of no surprise or of any plan. They didn't stay together I must say but throughout the years always finding one another along the way.

In spite of the daily tears and knowing Gods reason for the love so deep to be there through the years. And keeping still in knowing love finds them together as it always appears. Never gone too far away. The love is greater than all I must say.

So there is a piece of everyday that may or may not set our hearts or minds to get too carried away but, to find one's own peace even if it's only a hour out of a twenty-four

Always and forever having hope and faith but yet knowing the greatest is love.

The day drug on and on and I started feeling a little depressed so; I started in my writing and when I got to my revising well; it took a while and then I became quite impressed.

Thinking today how life passes through: many stages we may go through.

Some days very narrow and feeling crestfallen. Hoping the long road would soon end while; other days so pleasant yet brisk. Each day of our lives has its own meaning and way .i just try to remind myself and others to make it the best piece to fit in the most beautiful picture you will be staring right at someday. Though it will be a memory knowing than you will be at peace when the pieces of those memories are painted into a beautiful picture starting today and on in your own comfort.

It is now mid-August ans Summer is briskly moving right along.Not much impressed thinking of old man winter arriving soon and the idea of sometimes feeling depressed as the sun goes behind the gray clouds sometimes.

Eventhough the idea of the snow that does keep a sparkle and the footprints in the snow showing everywhere we go.

Our days are sometimes of a lighted candle in the wind not knowing sometimes when and if it may dim But; when we don't try so hard and just sit it at ease in a calming place you will find it will stay lit hour after hour. Bringing much peace just as putting our faith in God it is to be still in patience just as the candle light is still bringing much light and peace to our souls

Although I may seem to be a little too much ecclesiastically here, throughout my own life's lessons and experience I sure do ~~know~~ that God does walk with us and that love from him is the light that will never dim. Not one person is at all   perfect but, following our hearts and setting our minds on him. We were all born of his image and do have his holy spirit within us but, so many life's challenges and obstacles get in our way of the truth, that's when we allow them to by focusing on the negative aspects of our life allowing it to fully blind us in our peace and happiness and just sitting back searching for all the missing piece when we would just be still and see all along the pieces were there all along just waiting to be put back together bringing the most peaceful picture of all.

Leaving a dead end road left in destitution for many in so many ways when you just wave your hands in the air and say " I'm done" and trying to light your candle alone while walking against the Wind.

A new season is now at near. While I awake each morning in wishing you were here. I stare at the heavy snow on the tree limp with its bend as I ask myself why it all had to end. In spite of the doubts I battle through my head. My soul carries hope into every new sunrise reflecting all good vibes back off the mountain peaks.

The winter always so cold and dark only hearing all the wolves bark at the moon in hoping the ones they love will come back soon.

Although the heart may carry a wound this great love and strong soul keeps its self in amends' for many days .in hope you may find better ways out there on your inconclusive life's journey .

You must always remind yourself a true woman is a spiritual woman so when you have darkest days always look into the trees and find the brightest sun that rays and warms your thoughts and soul every step of the way

This here story should have been done But, as of for me being always on the run. Some days my thoughts being very unclear and other days my thought move me into the most beautiful atmosphere in a place called hope sometimes A must say it's usually just hearing the sounds of the ocean that carry me away.

As I write this with my eyes drooping I must finish later after a little recouping.

All the seasons come and go. Summer is quite warm and peaceful spring always being so fresh. And now autumn is here listening to the crunches of the colorful leaves that blow.

The birds singing loudly in a flock as they go on their way south leaving behind many seeds in love to just say they will return next May. The thoughts of winter being a little depressing for some clouds so dark and gray but always think of tomorrow each day when you pray.

So as the days often change and the seasons do to. People do   change as well. Some only at mind and some at heart too. Many just change their own minds and hold their loving part .or some just keep the change they made because their heart had sometime been torn apart by someone they love.

Sometimes it's not to know rather those feelings have changed or if the thoughts need rearranged in peaceful thinking to be left alone allowing peace in understanding. The feelings of others that have much confusion of their own often leave those who love them out in a big storm of confusion lost in hopes thoughts and dreams to believe in. just hanging on to an umbrella as if they just know it's going to be another rainy gray day, while many people hold on to all the hope and faith allowing the spirit of God's love

To shine down his warming love just as the warm sun will so always shine. Never running on any kind of empty lost in hope and to never be totally inconclusive of Gods better days for them.

    The evening is now here as the sounds of the big city is at a hush but; with thoughts of you in my mind at quite a rush.

    I sit in all silence and the only sound I hear is the peaceful sound from the train somewhere nearby and hoping you can hear it with me: wherever you are.

Sandcastles often get washed away just as tears do too, knowing there will always be many more, Just as the sun passes through the clouds of rain. Now knowing once again how everything is always ok by the end of the day when seeing the beautiful rainbow that is sent near after   all that's washed away

So building more sandcastles is where you'll often find me my love.

Maybe I will be sitting next to a white Dove.

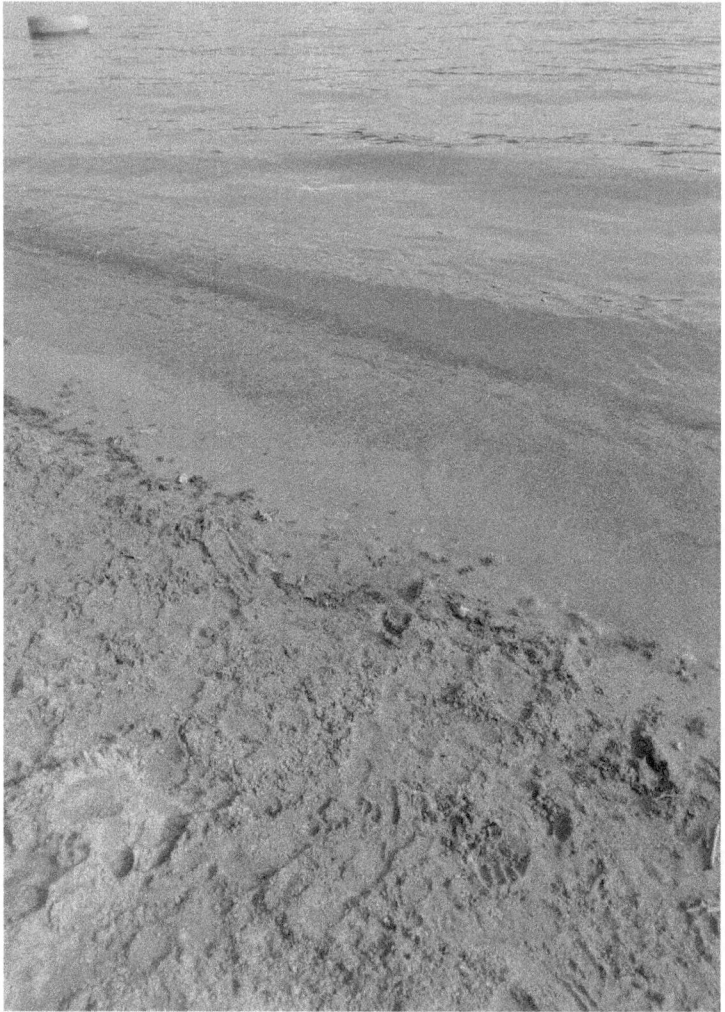

My unaccompanied visit to the lake to find
inspirational peace beside the water while thoughts
of you on my mind; in wishing you were here to find
the peace with me. September 17, 2017 Atwood lake
mineral city, Ohio

Also by, Grace Brand

Children's books

1--God made the big world

2-- AS big as me

Fairytale autobiographical fiction

Mermaid at heart

1st 2nd 3d editions

I can bring much peace to my ownself each day in hoping others do as well. Caputuring many positive thoughts through different outcomes and meaning each day brings. Moving my mind in the most positive direction .I am truly in
highest hopes you find much positive and greatest love in your own thoughts each day through this of my story I share with you and knowing of faith and hope but,yes the greatest is love.

Author, Grace Brand

$7.99
ISBN 978-1-7328694-2-4
50799

9 781732 869424

www.ingramcontent.com/pod-product-compliance
Lightning Source LLC
Chambersburg PA
CBHW021151020426
42331CB00005B/987